# The Edge of Everything

*poems by*

# Jo Bower

*Finishing Line Press*
Georgetown, Kentucky

# The Edge of Everything

Copyright © 2020 by Jo Bower
ISBN 979-8-89990-338-0 First Edition
All rights reserved under International and Pan-American Copyright Conventions. No part of this book may be reproduced in any manner whatsoever without written permission from the publisher, except in the case of brief quotations embodied in critical articles and reviews.

Publisher: Leah Huete de Maines
Editor: Christen Kincaid
Cover Art: Dina Crawford, SalisburySunrises.com
Author Photo: Jo Bower
Cover Design: Elizabeth Maines McCleavy

Order online: www.finishinglinepress.com
also available on amazon.com

Author inquiries and mail orders:
Finishing Line Press
PO Box 1626
Georgetown, Kentucky 40324
USA

# Contents

The Edge of Everything .................................................................. 1

**Growing**

I Grew Here ........................................................................... 5
Three-speed Memories ................................................................. 7
Maine Nights ......................................................................... 8
Ancestral Journeys ................................................................... 9
Matriarchs .......................................................................... 10
Queen of the Hill ................................................................... 11
Life Interrupted .................................................................... 12
Sisters Leaning ..................................................................... 13
Family Table ........................................................................ 14
Lake Carmi with My Daughter ......................................................... 15
Elegy for My Mother ................................................................. 16
ready to live ....................................................................... 17
Fortune Cookie Fallacies ............................................................ 18
Emergence ........................................................................... 20

**Exploring**

Wilderness Journey .................................................................. 23
How Can It Be? ...................................................................... 24
Rochester Gap ....................................................................... 25
Quietly Magnificent ................................................................. 26
question for the kayakers ........................................................... 27
Autumn Reveal ....................................................................... 28
golden falls ........................................................................ 29
Elemental ........................................................................... 30
Arrival at *Mothers' Acre* .......................................................... 31
Coming Home ......................................................................... 32

**Flowing**

Three from the Sea .................................................................. 35
Ocean at Salisbury Beach ............................................................ 36
Wave Dancers ........................................................................ 37
Coffee with the Whales .............................................................. 38
Elaine and Alden, Rowing ............................................................ 39
Joining the Ocean ................................................................... 40
Surfing My Body ..................................................................... 41

**Being**

    Teachable Feet ........................................................................... 45
    For My Beloved ......................................................................... 46
    Love Poem ................................................................................. 47
    Best Friends ............................................................................... 48
    On the Cusp .............................................................................. 49
    Original Song ............................................................................ 50
    Talking to Despair ..................................................................... 51
    Living with Your Dying ............................................................ 52
    Fear of Falling ........................................................................... 53

**Transforming**

    Unfurling Myself ....................................................................... 57
    Learning My Body Language ................................................... 58
    The Day I walked Out into the Sky—My Sojourn in West Africa ... 59
    None Ever Told Me How to Grow Old ................................... 61
    My Fifth Season in Three Parts ............................................... 62
    While Listening to *Sunrise Mass* ............................................ 65
    Seeking Fire ............................................................................... 66
    Traveler ...................................................................................... 67

    'No Egrets .................................................................................. 69

Prior Publication Credits ................................................................. 70
Acknowledgments ............................................................................ 71

*To Elaine MacGray Starrett*
*Mother, Artist and Lifelong Inspiration*

*and*

*Julie Ann Shaw, Beloved*
*Bringer of Light, Laughter and Love*

**The Edge of Everything**

I have learned
in my 70th year
my center is actually
at the edge
of everything.
No wonder I can't
keep my balance.
I see the world
from the edge,
where I could
so easily fall.

At the edge of everything
I, small beneath an infinite sky,
keep searching
for what is most deeply true.

# Growing

**I Grew Here**

I grew among the thistle weeds,
different from others
alone, gazing at the sea.
Wondering about the world beyond
my family,
overlooked by the world's standards,
days measured in hours,
days measured by doing expected things.

I grew at the horizon's edge,
imagining another journey
beyond my life and
the unfathomable sky above
where the relentless Atlantic
inspired me to reach for
what was most unlikely,
a gateway.

I grew here:
defied expectations
tore my own path
through weedy fields
where no one else went.

I grew here:
stopped trying
to fit onto manicured lawns
with monochrome schoolmates,
pompous ladies
sitting in the front pew.

I grew here:
spilled my heart's hidden pockets
onto blank pages.
I spoke again and again,
refused to be silent.

I grew here:
felt the sea pull
my words from a deeper place,
beneath waves to
hidden lairs
where my heart imagined freedom
and pathways to another life.

I grew here:
born of a roughhewn coast
my heart found answer
my poet found voice
beyond empty ocean
broken rocks.
I went my own way
unlimited by hours and days
found my place
in a world of abundant wonder
always waiting just for me.

**Three-speed Memories**

Freedom rose
                               in my wake
while wandering
                               vast back woods
behind my suburban home in
                               cutoff jeans and
sneakers in the widest
                               width my mom could find.
But ferns and woodchucks didn't care
                               that I walked funny
or stumbled on hidden roots.
                               My old three-speed took me
into the hills traversing trails
                               where no one saw my difference,
my crooked feet, my crooked mouth.
                               Up there I rode to the edge of exhaustion
rode and rode until the day overtook me.
                               One thousand private adventures
took me to a future
                               I alone would choose.

**Maine Nights**

The beds upstairs line up like sentries
all the bedspreads smoothed just so,
trunks of musty linens behind
where mice make cozy nests
for their little ones
once the humans vacate.

Even tired quilts are more than enough
to ward off summer night chill
as the dread nine o'clock horn rises from the deep dark.
Every night I snooze in shadowy
kerosene lamplight
squatting on the stairwell shelf.

Through knot holes in the floor
I glimpse the grownups downstairs
their voices soft and falling
heavy with coming sleep
all the windows open
to the black expanse outside the screens.

When I grew older, the night drew closer
cicadas serenaded me as I read for hours
on the worn couch downstairs
bathed in stillness
never wanting the mystical firelight
to go out.

## Ancestral Journeys

My father's people never knew comfort or care.
They carved towns out of logs and fallen brush.

Bore child after child after winter after spring,
forgotten names and places, Nova Scotia homesteads.

Great-grandmother planted carrots, tomatoes, and squash
for squalling babies and dirty-faced children.

My mother's people came from fishermen, pulling oars through gales,
steering home through storms, rocked by earthquake waves.

Grandmother's skirt billowed like clouds as she took my mother
from their hand-hewn cottage to Kittery's Sea Point by train.

My grandfather left his fishing village, turned to mending people,
a doctor who sternly disciplined his children with moral lessons.

Rules ingrained from hardscrabble years on the land's rough, untamed edge:
hard work, truthfulness and charity toward others.

The children are gone now, lost to life's inevitable ends,
only rotting shards of the railbed remain, fading signs of that seaside pilgrimage.

## Matriarchs

they draw us close
when birth ties fray break

they speak stillness
when restless winds blow us off course

they blow freedom
into locked, hidden places

they remain rooted
when we have flown to the sweet sky canopy

**Queen of the Hill**

I see you at six years old, poised on an icy slope,
new to the virgin snows of Vermont,
jumping on a piece of cardboard
mindless of the tree in your path.

Later, the dentist says you're lucky
you didn't expose a nerve
when the tree broke your tooth
but you've carried brokenness
across the years, trying to hide what
you've carried so long.

Finally, you yield to the logic of repair
though other scabbed-over sores remain, the crown
now planted in your mouth
confirms once and for all
you are Queen of the Hill.

## Life Interrupted
*For Tom*

I feel it, hundreds of miles away,
a loud thud echoes in my world
as my brother's life spills out
onto a city street, bicycle wheels spinning furiously.
He is a motionless heap on the sidewalk,
I fear I might lose him.
Doctors and machines return him
to us and the bonds
keep us living in rhythm
to the persistent beat of
family history, legacy
invisible, sometimes unwanted.

Bonds still hold us together,
branches of different shapes, sizes,
more and then less flexible.
Each of us pulls and pushes
on the raw truth
of our connection,
but in dissonant space
we join as one.

## Sisters Leaning

One on tiptoe
with long, lacy branches
slumping into the other's
arms of August fullness, with roots
half-pulled from the ground,
worn from the effort of quaking
under wind and rain.

Two aspen trees fixed in
common soil plain,
fallow, full of stones,
disintegrating plants.
One catching the other's
broken wings.

They pierce the lonely sky
with a plea, a prayer
for just one more season
to stand by the creek together
until, in time
they fall as one.

### Family Table

The long table had a beam beneath it
my legs never quite reached
unless I slouched, risking mother's wrath.
*Sit up*, she'd say with the slap of her voice,
promising a wooden spoon reminder.

The family table followed me through childhood
early rejections—with sobbing and sodden Kleenex -
forks, knives, napkins lined up.
I never found comfort in their order.
Crumbs from my life
\like brittle, cracking leaves
leaving only a messy floor
for someone to sweep away.

As I grew I sat there again
told stories of college escapades
overseas adventures
that left me forever changed
but wondering if it ever mattered.
My father sat heavy and loose with fatigue
while I made him breakfast on the days before Christmas
so I could sneak half a piece of bacon
and be daddy's little girl again.

At the family table
in the big, boisterous house
we made elaborate piñatas
for family parties
while children scrambled on the floor for treats
young adults swapped school stories
adults murmured *tsk tsk*
sipped eggnog while waiting for pie.

## Lake Carmi with My Daughter

Sitting behind you
in a low-slung kayak
I marvel at
swinging black braids
sliding down your back
shiny in the equinox sun.

Each stroke of dark water
reminds me of the nights
you swore you'd never go back
to fair weather lovers
whose loyalty proved
as shallow as lily pad roots.

Now, at the turning of our seasons together
as our lives intwine again
anchored in aging love, we turn as one
for the deep waters of Lake Carmi.

**Elegy for My Mother**

You are rowing
toward the light
against the tides
tethered to the sea,
*stroke, stroke*
c'mon mom you can do it, we cry
as we steady your boat.

But our voices dissolve
facing an icy sea,
our hands slowly, slowly
release their grasp on your gunwales.

You disappear behind the swells
but then appear again,
your face set and determined
to reach that farthest coast.
All your storms vanquished at last
you pull at the oars
refusing to stop until triumphant and true
you come to rest on the silvery shore.

**Ready to Live**

she is a woman
who came from downstairs going up
into her daughter's room
surveying the unmade bed, stains on the rug
leftovers from abandoned lovers
a lonely sock sticking out of the closet
as if to claim the stale, smoke-strangled air

she is a woman leaving behind
all that she was
discovering anew like a child
pure wonder of rocks
trees, leaves, streams
it was all here before she was
but truly
was she here all along

she is a woman remaking
her own mysteries
unrolling a new skein of she-magic
every day she opens her heart's door
once she thought the key forever lost
now she collects more than her hands can hold

she is a woman who
watched her mother's light
go out one winter morning
after, she let herself out the back door
entered a brand-new world
ready at last to live

## Fortune Cookie Fallacies

I never put much stock in
messages inside fortune cookies,
nor in my piano teacher, who often intoned,
*you'll have money when you die,*
as if the brown mole beside my mouth
decreed it so.

She tried to teach me all the major and minor scales
c, c-sharp, d-flat, d, d-sharp,
played at a furious pace up and down
the keyboard.

Much of my childhood was that way,
things were as they were
without reason or
explanation.

I was happy to leave childhood
Behind. I never cared for absolutes
or arbitrary anythings.

I finally stopped seeking
the fathers I would never have,
left their wallpaper ghosts whispering endlessly
about what they expected.

But I never forgave their inattention,
their assumptions about who I was and what I felt,
their unreliable love, which came and went,
came and went,
like the seaside seasons,
like report cards coming and going.

A grandmother, who gave up nursing
for her doctor husband and six children.

A mother, turning from her wild youth
to housewife life full of opinions, straight as
pine trees standing guard behind our house.

An aunt who pestered the young ones
pinching their cheeks, fawning and laughing,
enjoying their discomfort until
she was silenced by a stroke.

As for me, I travel my own path now
with companions only I select.
I am a fussy old woman,
picky about those I allow alongside
unwilling to temper my vision
for anyone. I have banished
fortune cookies, echoes of absent fathers,
as well as my piano teacher's pronouncements.

I am only myself.

**Emergence**

Clunky brown lace-up shoes
scuffed on the soles
wedges glued on to
keep wobbly feet in line.
Their grip on most surfaces
tenuous on the best days,
never mind the worst.

I wanted to hide in the shadows.
Nothing ever fit:
shoes—too narrow
sneakers—too flimsy
dresses—too small
tears—too weak
emotions—too big
shame—too constant.

But over time, the shadows disappeared,
replaced by sheer stubbornness.
A warrior was born
and a new journey began.

# Exploring

**Wilderness Journey**

Begin
as I step onto paths
only imagined before
or seen in Vermont travel books
each turn awaits its reveal, whether farmland expanse
or narrow roads zigzagging through mountains.

See
this rugged land, once strange, now familiar
though rocks and fallen oak trees half-hide yellow sweetgrass,
other wildflowers, names unknown, pop with color
through landscapes I am mapping.

Listen
to wild, high love keening from the river's edge, maybe loons, maybe crows
or perhaps a woman weeping,
I have never ventured this far
fearing lament without end.

Feel
my lover slip her hand into mine
grey hair cascades peace
spills into every last pore
creates safety in the hilly wilderness.

Arrive
home following well-trod paths
a fire warm in my heart and chili on the stove
pull a plain shawl around our lives
time to rest, sleep.

Dream
of tomorrow's paths inviting
their outlines engraved on our bones
undisturbed, waiting for our footfalls
still exploring this place
as only wild things do.

## How Can It Be?

How can it be?
that my soul sinks into
the hollows of this place
as if it has always habited here.

How can it be?
that I so easily add layers of living
to accommodate the suddenly
shifting seasons
after a lifetime of flat city dwelling.

How can it be?
that my feet find purchase
on pebbly, worn shores
where wild birds and bears
come to breed and feed.

How can it be?
that words born in this space
spring and sprout with wild abandon
years after I thought writer's muse had gone.

How can it be?
that after years of moving through too many spaces
carrying the concrete weight
of yearning for a different life
that I find myself here, in the place I was always meant to be.

How can it be?

**Rochester Gap**

Spring light
slides through the late afternoon,
endless screens of trees.

Glimpses of the pine needle carpet
now glowing with early spring sun slanting,
slicing the sleeping soil.

Vibrant hues now lime, now seafoam, now fern
emerge from barren branches, brown and grey
stepping up the hillside to absorb stubborn snow patches.

Rochester Gap rides the embrace of wild mountains
trees join their long arms above
low bundled buds burst to life.

Waters race in unfettered streams
with resounding ripples that remember
ancient awakenings in lakes and ponds.

Their ride continues
to the sea where all life began
waving to the whales from the waterfall.

Sinking into the sharp shiny brine
the sandy shore greets
every last drop returning home.

**Quietly Magnificent**

What can be said
about the coming of spring?

The way dark red wine buds
color the treetops as I pass,

slender greens
push dead weeds aside.

Sunlight shines through lazy haze
promising more hours between afternoon and twilight.

Short sleeves sprout
on the arms of running children.

My mouth widens its smile
as I behold the earth awake.

**question for the kayakers**

shimmering shards of light
shake themselves awake
butterflies held captive by the sun

two orange kayaks close together
interrupt the rippling, radiant water
slide silently through swelling ripples

they strive to match
their dipping paddles
to meet the rising currents and wind

seen from the shore
they pull against prevailing breezes paddles
rise and rise again

what will they learn
when the wind dies away
and they float alone in stillness

**Autumn Reveal**

dark stars fall
reveal inner light
as summer runs away
like an escaping beachball
the leaves' true color
pop to view
yellow, orange, red
too bright for earth-bound eyes
the morning breaks open
with a noteless symphony
the wind catches
dark stars falling
makes a bed
where safe and secure
my lover and I
will dream
a white winter
away

**golden falls**

leaves let go twirl to earth
fantastic parachutes carrying color
from sky to sodden ground
pine needles caress my neck like a lover

spines of ancient serpentines rise
out of the ground crisscross the berm
witness another year's turning summer to winter
but not before laying a carpet of gold

no human eyes will watch that falling
from this bench it is mine alone
blues rise as gold falls strip their hosts bare but for their essence
standing silent sentry through the long winter
as forest scavengers seek food when their stores run thin

meanwhile golden falls continue
casting a spell upon blue water while leaves drop
drift languidly until claimed by the bog
disappearing underground to nest for a new generation
watery bed for new life springing
as seasons turn as seasons must

the geese have gone in their collective Vs
leaving one lonely pair to fight the winter
finding solace in the crevice between tree trunks
haven enough for two

### Elemental

Under the snow-weighted branch
the white sheen of a million snowflakes
mirrors a still center.
There is nothing here except
the single, sky-blue moment
holding time gingerly
like a newborn.

Throw open the gates to the universe
grant freedom time
to fly beyond the edges
of a tired earth.

Sparks from a bonfire at night
rise to melt the world's ice
becoming summer fireflies
swarming the sky's horizon.

**Arrival at *Mothers' Acre***

We came there
bearing used-up dreams and weary hopes
for paradise
as a shallow stream wandered by,
weaving our gains and losses
into an exquisite web.

'
Lifetimes intertwined
we dug into the mountain
laid our wisdom down,
seeds for our children.

*Mothers' Acre:*
where our past times,
unknowable futures
rested peacefully—two crones
spooned on a camp mattress
as choirs of peepers
sent their serenades
steady and sonorous
into the dark.

## Coming Home

I fall upward
an unforgettable
waking dream
swallowed by
streams, swallows, searing sunsets, by
lakes, morning light, loons, by
spirit, and spilling colors, scarlet skies.

Every twig speaks
its own true name,
marks the time of
unfolding, unfurling,
bursting from winter cocoon
exploding to wild shouts,
splashing everywhere.

Fledglings snuggle near
their mothers
unafraid of tomorrow's
solo flight.

Rest now until
sunlight rises,
paints the horizon,
points the way
for all living things
to rise and fly as one,
splitting the night open,
scattering millions of stars.

Images of essence,
lasting legacies for generations
to come.

**Flowing**

# Three from the Sea

*What I have left behind has not left me.*—David Whyte

## 1-Remains

of sticky saltiness wake me with a jolt
though I am far away,
in a place slow to wake from
winter, distant from any beach.

Unforgettable images
wash through me,
like comforting dreams,
taking me to tender places.

Returning me
again and again
to where my life truly began.

## 2-Gratitude

fills my pores with
sharp, salty bites of air
blown about in early light.

As a perfect morning passes,
slow-moving pendulum of
light and shadow chase
across beach expanses.

My heart sings in this place
when all else changes
or fades away.

## 3-Beachcombing

memories stick to my feet
though I departed the coast long ago
odd seashells and sea glass shards
cradled carefully in a plastic bag
for the long trudge home.

## Ocean at Salisbury Beach

Facing
calm, blue waters,

I witness the sea, comforted by
its foaming unfurling onto the sand.

Feel breezes
across my bare arms.

I drink in the light
of an expanding sunrise.

Sea birds flap
their way to feed.

Brightness appears beneath
elongating red streaks across the sky.

Life etches
its ebbs and flows

onto my heart's calendar,
directs my feet

where to stand in uncertain times
sets me free.

Light for the world appears
just as it did yesterday,

just as it will do again
tomorrow.

## Wave Dancers

### I

Clouds in the sunrise sky open, invite thin slits of light to widen
spread downward, illuminate each breaking wave.

White diamonds bounce atop ebbing tides
glistening, glimmering in early morning light.

Overhead, crows compete for one singular spot on a brick chimney
squat, then soar through wind, sky.

Crows rise, then dip to land in a different spot,
strange, no bird claims the best view, the edge closest to the sea.

Beside a blackened fire pit, shards of dull brown glass encircle it,
glowing iridescent, mirror a fading sky.

### II

Men load pristine sands into dump trucks, make way for motels,
swimming pools, grinding gears foretell the coming of more people
and cars, more dollars.

Mechanical diggers expose the places worms hide from the cycling
tides, marsh grasses give way to squishing work boots.

But what of the crows who still seek the relentless churn of the waves,
the constant turn of the seasons on this sea-bound strip of land?

Wild water meets itself, wafting upward to create cloud clusters,
now merging into one, now parting again, only to send more white
diamonds down.

## Coffee with the Whales

scanning with
outdated binoculars
I want to have coffee
with the Blues
watch them leap, breach
in the sparkling waves
run my hand along
their flanks, scarred by fishlines
breathe in their tales of
icebergs in Canada
warmer winds on the Outer Banks
and other, more distant dreams
diving for more delectable treats
growing in the blue-green brine
communing with porpoises
starfish and sharks
soaking in the sea's goodness
with the strong pull of the moon
unseen but undeniable
the whales roll over
in morning's white blaze
and I am with them
losing sight of land

**Elaine and Alden, Rowing**

Stroking on the edge of the sea
from where I first glimpsed you
heading toward that silvery shore.

Stroking on the edge of the sea
from where you bade farewell
to your lover as the bugle played taps
for the man who made music
in your heart with his trombone.

Stroking on the edge of the sea
I see you rowing together
with long, rhythmic lines
tethered to the sea.

Stroking on the edge of the sea
from where you put your oars in endless waters
I witness you crossing
to the silvery shore
certain of your destination
beyond the breaking waves.
you and your lover
laughing and loving
and rowing.

**Joining the Ocean**

Facing out
toward calm, blue waters.

Breezes cross my bare arms,
raise hairs, turn skin vaguely pink.

Below my ocean of anxiety,
the waves slap the rocks like a fist.

Sea birds languidly flap
their way to lunchtime feeds.

Life etches its ebbs and flows
onto my heart's calendar.

Directs my feet
to stand strong in uncertain times.

My arms become wings, send me flying
to the sea.

**Surfing My Body**

Incoming tide
takes me by surprise,
slopping over
sneaker-bound toes
baptizing them with fading waves.

    Suddenly, I'm the child
    racing toward the waves
    in utter delight,
    waiting for just the right one
    as the tide approaches.
    I see it come, breaking.
    It carries me,
    weightless, breathless, arms and legs askew,
    until I land on wet sand,
    rise up to surf my body again.

Even now at 70, to walk the beach
still a delicious pleasure,
crutches under my arms
legs of flesh and metal.

Somehow, I still feel whole.

# Being

**Teachable Feet**

In the beginning,
these feet were desolate
toes curling under
in mute embarrassment
jealous of the ballet dancer's long, strong sole
with high arches walking
in all the fanciest shoes
heels, dressy boots, loafers
gliding through life
precisely balanced.

These feet learned much, much later
they alone did not have to carry the body.
See, they are planted, without much effort
on the flattest floor—heel to toe.
Surprise—hips and ass
can be conscripted to provide stability, sturdiness
enough to carry a body, safely, through space.

## For My Beloved

We sit close
in a great concert hall
a hundred pulsing voices surround us.

Your soul flies high,
communes deeply
with overtures and finales.

You are here,
eyes closed,
wrapped in passionate bliss.

I behold you
as beautiful, as holy
as I have ever seen you.

And my heart
will never be
big enough to hold you.

## Love Poem

I am certain
even when you go
you will be bound to me.
I will never exist apart from you,
love has blasted past
all the boundaries we assume
separate us.

Our bond will be
bright blue like the sea,
bright blue like your eyes,
bright blue like all
the memories we will gather
like sea glass through our lives.

Thick and tough
the cord will be our guarantee
what we created will endure beyond
life, death, imagination and more.
A promise never broken
will tether my soul to yours
forever.

**Best Friends**

My beloved and her best friend
sit close in the front seat.
Time and distance fall away,
reveal a sisterhood undisturbed by
miles and time zones apart.
You found a way to erase the space.
Today I witness the full flower
of your years-long friendship, aging with you
and bask in its reflected glow.

**On the Cusp**

Smoke swirls and disappears
into crackling cold air,
blue sky blinding
with infinity's impossible purity.

Disappearing behind trees, hills
dancing, bedazzling the wind
whispering of warmer days to come.

The muse sleeps—then startles awake
to gales of passion, rage, sadness,
emotions billow up abruptly as
sudden gusts of words
scatter like late snowflakes.

Serenity splits open and vaporizes
in mid-sentence, gravity relents and
mountains tumble upward,
night plummets, obscuring
every last flickering light.

When the storm passes
she comes to the page at last
ready to tame the wild things
too big to capture, corral or tame,
too small to cup in her hand.

Words emerge as mixed voices
chords on her inner piano
solos and sonnets in minor keys
clouds of words rising
sinking into her heart
bound together as one.

It's time to
reassemble shards
of the fading season
recreate a vessel to launch anew
the incomparable blooms
of a returning Spring.

## Original Song

facing blank pages as snow outlines
black asphalt ribbons

along this solitary street
the clock hands turn back

where is the way forward beside wooded trails
where my legs no longer carry me

I find myself beginning here
at what I thought was life's ending

I sink deep into endless leaf layers
on the edge of my own wilderness

moving through dense undergrowth
rediscovering my restless self

an abrupt snow squall rolls down the mountain
separated by a thinning curtain from bone-deep wisdom

can I be free enough to sing its essence

## Talking to Despair

Where does despair live in my body?
I imagine it, microscopic
creature swimming in blood,
from little toe to the top of my head.

Most often lingering in the shadows
between the vertebrae in my back
reminding me of the price paid for holding my
large, round body upright
atop spindly legs surgically altered to
appear *normal* to schoolchildren, once and
later, to adults whose long strides still outpaced my own.

All the attempts to make my body
look and work normally were in vain.
Though I didn't learn this until many years later,
years lost feeling like an outcast
even after multiple surgeries,
a summer outside in the chaise lounge,
my legs encased in plaster.

I don't remember friends coming over,
only the reliable escape into
imaginary play close by the lawn,
once lushly green, then turning brown,
on days when rain stayed away
as if afraid to catch my deformity
like a creeping virus coming out
of the woods to pounce.

It was an endless summer that year,
when modern medicine
denied me the release of swimming pools,
backyard games, replaced by unwelcome
memories, the stink of ether,
being carried upstairs at bedtime.

## Living with Your Dying

Your body
is slipping
to a far place.
I can't stop
your slowing down,
your awkward stumble.
You keep going.
Stubbornness streaks
through every step,
leaves you shaken,
exhausted.

The sky today,
translucent, bright.
I see nothing
beyond white haze.

You are slipping
through a hole
in the sky.
I cannot follow.

No words for your regrets.
Believing you failed
those close to you.
Your moan
slips through seamed lips.

*Hold onto the good,*
I whisper.
But you only slip further away.

I don't know how to live
in this world
without you.

**Fear of Falling**

> *...I want to know if you know*
> *how to melt into that fierce heat of living*
> *falling toward*
> *the centre of your longing....*
> —David Whyte

Where is the center of my longing:
Is it in Vermont's endless expanse of lakes and woods?
Is it on a blank page waiting for words to give it life?
Is it in the laughter of my beloved, making yet another raucous joke?
Is it in 2 a.m. silence when I cannot sleep?

I have not yet dug deep enough into the soil of my soul
but muse is calling me there
to the space where all passions dance.

But how can I let myself fall when the ground is harsh, rough, rocky?
Can I bear the pain of what it will take to rise from such a steep drop?

I am not yet ready to fall toward the center of my longing,
imagining I will only find emptiness,
disappointment there; finally overcome by
failing to shape poems after
the most authentic version of me.

Yet my truest self waits to be lit,
become a bonfire of hopes and fears,
challenges met and challenges failed.
Life full beyond any telling of it.
Wisdom found in dark and light places.
I wait for that one moment
to fall toward the center of my longing.

# Transforming

**Unfurling Myself**

in the face of a gale
unfurling myself
despite the dangers of
flying off my feet
into unseen chasms beneath Lake Champlain

I also see tulips, other buds
as I await the storm
knowing for certain
a glorious, exploding Spring
is coming

**Learning My Body Language**
    For Jackie

For over half a lifetime
my body's language felt strange
as I flailed against it.
Only in water did my body
begin to respond as I wanted.

Then you came: student of bodies,
attending each part; strong, weak,
smooth, scarred.

You knew the language of my body
though it was only a murmur, nearly inaudible,
distorted neurons lost in mazes with no exit.

You taught me
I could come home to my body,
give it space, honor it, even revel in it
and to my surprise, learn from it.

**The Day I Walked Out Into The Sky—
My Sojourn in West Africa**

I left home without a parachute,
I didn't know I was going on this trip
leaving solid ground behind.

I only had a passport,
a change of clothes
with only a few words pronounced
with strange sounds sticking in my throat.

I didn't know I was leaving my old self
at New York's bustling airport
only to find a new self there
on a dusty, noisy, smelly airfield
where we had to lug our bags
across a steamy tarmac.

Many black bodies pressed
against mine, shouting, looking frantically
for a rich foreigner's fare,
finally finding the van that would take us
away from the city, down dusty red roads
past thickets of palm trees
into a wildness I never imagined.

There were buildings and houses and
schedules on this remote college campus.
But a ten-minute walk
through flowering vegetation taller than I
parted just enough for a narrow track,
sent me out into the bush,
then returned me to the place
I had started.

I barely knew the place
though I basked in midnight massages and
whispered secrets, even learning
a new kind of love in
this strange, foreign place.

It was a time like no other:

finding friendship and forging friendly bonds
with handshakes ending in finger snaps,
punctuating the coming and going
of comrades,
witnessing sunsets filling
the late day sky from
horizon to horizon
color heaped upon color
a giant shifting kaleidoscope,
every imaginable color
bidding farewell to the day
in a most spectacular way.

When my adventure was done
I left there with red dirt sticking to all
my innermost places
knowing I would never use my old
eyes to see the world again.

Today my heart is populated by
the lessons of that place,
where wildness holds the upper hand
and war has rent the landscape,
where people struggle to survive,
where my heart learned there are no true boundaries.

It was there I finally felt home,
an unlikely place, where people reached me
with their hearts and hopes
gave me a way to be in the world
with outstretched hands, ready to welcome
strange, red roads and impossibly massive sunsets
and other landscapes I have yet to explore
but have no need to fear.

**No One Ever Told Me How to Grow Old**

My mother and I never discussed it:
the older women in my family
were frumpy,
had a mean streak
borne from lives of forced compliance.

Once old, it seemed their cronehood sanctioned
critical words, cutting judgements.
My mother chaffed at her sisters' aging unkindness,
my younger brother wilted beneath it,
all of us hated it.

So I used Covid
to spring into aging:
launching myself into a canopy of trees,
spilling words into rivers,
watching them climb to the clouds,
fly to the sea and knew with clarity
there was no turning back.

## My Fifth Season in Three Parts

I

Some days I don't recognize myself.

I have slid from one sort of wisdom
to another,
from child's sandbox to crone's wisdom,
from office walls to unfurling murals of oceans,
striding across mountains.
I carry words and visions
searching for a place to claim.

What used to be present
is now past,
the window of memory swings both ways.

Days melt into one another like seasons
butter and eggs on a hot pan
or soup emulsifying in the pot,
all flavors find their place
pleasuring my palate.

Suddenly it's my fifth season.
I am newly cocooned in mountains and rivers,
streams, lakes, sunsets.

I have grown unexpected wings,
learning to my surprise
I already know how to fly.

**II**

Suspended between summer and fall
as the last leaf falls
I am captive to this one
exquisite exceptional moment
time stops under the muted canopy.

The wonder of Lincoln Gap
opens first above
peeking blue through early yellow leaves,
then below, noisy streams rushing to rest
before winter freezes them in place.

Then ahead, turning a corner
late summer wonders
reveal air, sharply pungent.
I could inhale raw beauty
through every last pore
forever.

## III

Chasing gossamer
and golden threads of wonder
but waking cold.

All I can hear are
blunted fragments from dreams
denied and unremembered.

Drowning in dark memories
submerged in grief
I stroke for the surface.

Yet the land's contours emerge
from winter white sleep
as days turn longer, claw back sunlight.

Maybe tomorrow's sunrise
brimming suddenly with spring
will reveal radiant mountain peaks
lush valley meadows
nudging the thread of wonder awake.

## While Listening to *Sunrise Mass* by Oja Gjeilo

### Moment

Sunrise awakes spring leaves,
white light shimmers on green canopies.
Tiny earthworms,
once dormant underground,
break the soil,
emerge to sun's spring brilliance.

### She Sings with Her Hands

Slowly and now faster

      rising

            falling

                    swaying.

Keeping time with
ancient masters
performing in her
living room

    notes vibrate

           many voices

                  fill the space.

All shadows now vanquished
her hands fall
to her lap
echoes repeat and resound.

## Seeking Fire

Where is my fire?
some days, it pushes me to the edge
of a burning field.

To watch, mesmerized as
yellowed, wild grasses
turn angry orange.

I am driven to turn thoughts
into words that burn pure,
clearing my own forest path.

Away from falseness
emerging to light
a lasting legacy of truth.

Yet sometimes my fire seems to
sleep nearly forgotten,
beneath layers of everyday living.

Mixed memories of family
once anchored my days
now they sleep upstairs in an old spool bed.

But I remember
summer fires flickering
in a Maine fireplace.

I remember dark pines
watching over childhood play.
I remember their sapling offspring.

Today, grown past maturity,
the tall ones droop with fatigue,
aged and heavy with pine cones.

Yet they still shelter
dreams of creating
my own field of fire.

## Traveler

Is it wisdom I seek or truth?
and if truth, whose?
The one learned by my childhood self
forever trapped in boring saddle shoes?
Or the one imagined by my spirit,
dancing through cultures far different from mine?

To find the origins of my wild, wandering self
I travel through my lifetime
dive into my wildness
descend to the bottom.

Altogether different, even alien
I always knew myself to be *other*, outsider.
Seeking without ceasing
a name truly my own.

This one word still eludes me,
my true calling from the universe comes slowly
on the journey spiraling in
from a starry night in a lakeside campground,
to a kayak, paddling with my daughter.

But as I travel further,
this I know for sure:
my compass is true.

## No 'Egrets

Sometimes I want the world to disappear. There are too many questions to answer and to ask:
all these queries are way too numerous even with a lifetime to answer, especially in the later years when words can be elusive.

I am tempted to visit the fantasy world of *what ifs:*

> *what if* I had married my college boyfriend?
> *what if* I had given birth to one or more children?
> *what if* I had abandoned school to cross Africa with a bunch of strangers?

There is nothing of interest here.

I have a saying, *no 'egrets,* which came to me on Maine's Scarborough Marsh as I sat mesmerized by an active colony of egrets, awed by their breathtaking grace and freedom. I will never forget what it was like to watch them and become one with them. Through those hours, I joined them, filled with the wonder of those wild flying things.

## Prior Publication Credits

| | |
|---|---|
| *Lake Carmi with My Daughter* | Tiny Seed Literary Journal [online], 2024. |
| *Elegy for My Mother* | Silver Birch Press [online], 2024 and Wingless Dreamer, *Growth in Grief*, 2024. (formerly titled *You are Rowing*) |
| *Three-speed Memories* | Montpelier Poem City, 2024, [public display and print anthology]. |
| *Living with Your Dying* | Wingless Dreamer, *Soulful Verses*, 2023. |
| *On the Cusp* | Wingless Dreamer, 2023. |
| *Teachable Feet* | Wingless Dreamer, 2023. |
| *Rochester Gap* | Montpelier Poem City, 2023 [public display & print anthology]. |
| *Autumn Reveal* | Poem Town, Randolph (VT), *Poem Town Anthology*, 2023. |
| *How Can It Be?* | Montpelier Poem City, 2022, [public display]. |
| *Our Last Day* | Academyoftheheartandmind.com [online], 2021. |

## Acknowledgments

I have been inspired beyond words by Vermont's lovely landscape, and the many warm and wonderful friends I have made since coming here.

Specifically, I am eternally grateful to Valerie Bacharach of Pittsburgh PA and author of *Lost Glimpse* and *Ghost-Mother*. Her faith in my writing and her skills as a close reader have been instrumental in bringing this book to life.

I am also deeply grateful to Laurie McMillan (Flagstaff, AZ), friend, poet and teacher, who introduced me to a fabulous writers' community in Vermont and has provided invaluable guidance and support for my writing journey.

For friendship and counsel on how best to structure this book and ways I might market it, as well as help designing a web page, I am especially appreciative of my friend Lily Hinrichsen (Bristol VT), poet and fiber artist, who has freely shared her knowledge, as well as tips on where to find the best thrift shops in Vermont.

I knew from the beginning that my work would benefit from being viewed by many "early eyes." For giving so generously of their time and constructive feedback, I acknowledge Cynthia Liebermann, Sb Sowbel, Anita Mallinger and Caroline Donnan, members of a small and powerful writing critique group which met 2021 to 2024.

I would be remiss if I didn't thank all my dear friends from the Monday night group. Although our group's name changes frequently, your love and support has always been there and means the world to me.

And finally, without a doubt, this book would not have been created without the steadfast care and love of my beloved, Julie Ann Shaw.

**Jo Bower**, a lifelong activist and writer, identifies as a lesbian and person with disabilities. For as long as she can remember, she has always wanted to help others and make a difference in the world.

Born in Ohio, she moved to a small Massachusetts seaside community at age 12 where she fell in love with the craggy coast and chilly waters of New England.

She was first drawn to writing in adolescence, with encouragement from her English teacher and her first writing mentor. They recognized and supported not only her creative writing, but also her skills of keen observation, questioning and chronicling the world around her.

These interests, coupled with a strong streak of curiosity, led her to Kalamazoo College in Michigan, known for its expansive foreign study program. Her fascination with cultures different from her own led her to three months of study at Cuttington College, a liberal arts college nestled in inland Liberia, an experience that profoundly touched and changed her view of the world.

Inspired by her travel to Africa, she secured a one-year internship with the South African Associated Newspapers, [no longer in existence] a liberal chain of daily papers where she worked in Johannesburg and Cape Town and spent three months assisting at the association's bureau in Zimbabwe's capital.

Upon return to the US, Bower had a short career as a beat journalist on the North Shore of Massachusetts but soon felt called to a career in human services.

Relocating to the Boston area, Bower worked for many different non-profits, eventually earned her MSW at the Boston University School of Social Work (with a concentration in human services management) and eventually worked as an advocate and program developer for the Northeast Independent Living Program in Lawrence, MA, promoting dignity and independent living for all people with disabilities.

Throughout her career, Bower met the multiple challenges of family, children and increasing professional responsibility. Upon retirement, she returned to writing, her first love, and moved to Vermont. Today she thrives in a nourishing community of fellow writers. Bower and her cat Junebug live near Montpelier, VT.

Bower's poems have appeared in *Tiny Seed Journal* [online], Wingless Dreamer publications, *Down in the Dirt* [online] anthologies, and *Poem City Montpelier (2022 - 2025)*. *The Edge of Everything* is her first book.

www.ingramcontent.com/pod-product-compliance
Lightning Source LLC
Chambersburg PA
CBHW030056170426
43197CB00010B/1554